TRANSITIONING INTO PURPOSE

IMANI FAITH MOORE

Copyright © 2020 TRANSITIONING INTO PURPOSE:

All rights reserved. No part of this publication may be reproduced, stored in a retrieval system, or transmitted in any form or by any means—for example, electronic, photocopy, recording—without the prior written permission of the author and/or publisher. The only exception is brief quotations in printed reviews.

ISBN: 978-1-949461-19-0

The book recounts certain events in the life of Imani Faith, according to her recollection and perspective. The goal of the stories provided are not to defame any person or image or organization, but the sole purpose is to encourage and empower the reader to embrace change and grow because of it.

TRANSITIONING INTO PURPOSE

Dedication

I dedicate this project to all of my ancestors near and far.

With a special dedication to my Mama and Daddy

Mama Colette Mawusi and Yahshua Ben Israel, I thank you for being my very first teachers and spirit guides. I thank you for laying the foundation and planting the seed so that I may seek understanding as it relates to life's purposeful existence through the exposure of a Pan African Cultural environment, in addition to the religious, cosmic, and philosophical aspects of life. Ultimately, I thank you for the many life experiences and sacrifices made. You both unknowingly paved the way in creating and leaving a legacy intended to be reverberating for generations. Lastly, I thank you for the overload of love, encouragement, discipline, knowledge, and wisdom that has impacted and made the vision and completion of this project possible.

LOVE,

~Imani Faith ♥♥

Imani Faith

Acknowledgements

I am that I am God, Creator of Heaven, and Earth: Thank you for blessing me with the time, energy, and patience to carry out the divine plan to share my spiritual journey through my writing.

Naikwayah, my ace and firstborn. I was blessed to give birth to you at the very young age of 16, and I am more than grateful to say that you are indeed my greatest accomplishment. I thank you for being the motivating force to go further than I could have ever imagined.

D'Jaton, my only man child: Your birth is what truly caused me to begin pushing past what was expected of me. I pray that you will allow my journey to navigate you through life's unexpected obstacles and encourage you to live life as if you are confidently knowing that you are made in God's image and likeness. Therefore, nothing or no one can defeat you at reaching your highest potential.

Iyana, my true mini-me: You're such a beautiful soul that was birthed from my womb according to God's divine timing. I thank you for allowing me to teach you things through my experiences that the world cannot teach you. I thank you for gifting me with your amazing sense of humor, inquisitive nature, and efflorescence swag.

Sunette, my sunshine, my sister, my God-given life partner, the only sibling our mother chose to birth using another one of our father's seeds: Thank you for assisting me in pushing past the pain, disappointment, and many experiences to help me become the woman I am today. I pray that the bond between us never grows old but will remain full of life. Know that I will forever love you unconditionally and cherish the fact that you are the best accountability partner a girl could ever ask for.

TRANSITIONING INTO PURPOSE

Special Thanks:

Sometimes we are blessed with people who come into our lives for a period of time, reason or season. The timing is perfectly aligned according to God's divine purpose for our lives, and for that, I am truly grateful.

Tanishia, my best friend and soulmate: Thank you for traveling along my journey for many years, inspiring me to look deeper within SELF, not knowing that the learning experiences in which we shared would one day be used to heal what was once considered to be unknown.

Carol Bryant, my bonus Mama: Thank you for birthing a man-child who later became the man that God would place in my path making it possible for me to give life to a beautiful baby girl, making up the perfect combination of both of us. I thank you for your love, support, and unwavering presence in your granddaughter's life, for it will never go unnoticed and I will forever be grateful.

Jerri, Kadidra, Kiyaa: You are all the true definition of a kindred spirit. My sistah's, my childhood friends, my accountability partners, my business partners, my coaches, my healers, my spiritual readers, and confidants. Words can't express the gratitude I feel when it comes to the presence of each of you in my life. I thank the ancestors daily for our perfect, whole, and complete alignment as it relates to the unbreakable bond and connection that was intended for us to forever have.

Raminiyah Ingram, my spiritual doula, mentor, and emotional lifesaver: Thank you for helping me look beyond what appeared to be my reality. Thank you for your guidance in helping me to let go of people, things, and experiences that no longer served a purpose in my life. Thank you for helping me understand the true power of energy, alignment, and spirit. Thank you for being the ultimate motivating force in writing this book.

Imani Faith

Blank pages are intentional

TRANSITIONING INTO PURPOSE

Contents

Introduction 9

Chapter 1: Transitions 15

Chapter 2: Resurrection Time 65

Chapter 3: Divine Infinite Intelligence 77

Chapter 4: Planting Seeds 87

Chapter 5: Everything Always Works Out For Me 97

Chapter 6: Faith Is 103

Chapter 7: Seasons 111

Contact the Author 120

TRANSITIONING INTO PURPOSE

TRANSITIONING INTO PURPOSE

Introduction

Purpose has been a question pondered for generations. To give a glimpse of relatable life changing experiences that assisted me in identifying my own purpose, I decided to write it all down. By sharing my moments of reflection, I hope that as you are enduring your own transitions, or previous ones, that you can use this book as a reminder for the progress in which you have already made.

In addition, I hope that you utilize this tool to maintain your momentum as you endure the highs and lows of life. If you feel stuck, stuck in a moment, a situation, a relationship, a place or season, or are in the place of the unknown, I challenge you to move beyond your comfort zone to experience the process of growth.

Imani Faith

It is significant for you to consider turning a cheek at what you were once taught. I want you to tap into your thoughts, feelings and actions during each and every moment of uncertainty going forward.

Overall, I want you to know that there is cause and effect in everything that we do and experience from birth to death. However, once we become of age, we can choose to live the rest of our days walking in the path of what is expected, or we can choose to expand our God given sense of awareness; therefore, assuming the responsibility to purposely get the most out of this thing called life.

TRANSITIONING INTO PURPOSE

Finally, here are some key points and things I want you to know:

- This is *your* year of vision.
- It's time to develop an agenda for *your* own life.
- The time for *your* breakthrough is now.
- It's important for you to be ready to break free from chains of poverty, low self-images, and defeat.
- Lastly, commit to examining and reexamining yourself so you can emerge as a better, stronger, greater version of yourself. You were created by the Creator to **CREATE**.

Imani Faith

BOOK LAYOUT:

In this text, I provide some insight regarding the pursuit of purpose. Incorporating thoughts from respected authors that have helped me over the years as well as sharing some of my own journey. At the opening of each chapter, I provide a "Things To Consider" section that will have a challenge question, an affirmation and will list the respective suggested crystal for that chapter. Later, towards that end of chapter I incorporate poetry that my mother penned throughout the years which in some cases, gives further revelation to what is previously written. The last section is more interactive. O called it "Peaceful Practice. These are various practices that I hope that you would implement in your own life once this book is complete.

TRANSITIONING INTO PURPOSE

The lessons I learned from my parents as well as my life experiences, have been somewhat legendary for me. I hope some of the gems of wisdom I have collected will also be beneficial for you. Let's dig in!

Imani Faith

TRANSITIONING INTO PURPOSE

1
TRANSITIONS[1]

In any given moment, I can choose to return to peace.

THINGS TO CONSIDER:

Challenge Question/Statement: In what ways has transition impacted your life? Record them on a separate sheet now.

Affirmation: Change is inevitable, but my strength is too!

Healing Crystals: Black, Clear and Pink Calcite

Transitions are an unavoidable part of life. These inescapable happenings that stretch us beyond our capacities are something that we can all take a second to learn more about. Transitions are defined as the following according to Randy G. Fine:

> *a. Uncomfortable ends followed by hopeful new beginnings.*
>
> *b. The way the universe gives us the lessons we need to learn and keeps us on the paths that are best for us.*

---

[1] Inspired by: Yahshua Ben Israel and Mama Mauwsi

> c. A positive process we can trust and an opportunity for rebirth.

While I've always wanted to write a book, I never realized that some of the most intense times of my own transitions would be the times where I would experience the most growth.

Hence, in this project, I share some of my most significant life transitions in addition to some very significant principles learned along the way by providing a brief description of highly recommended healing crystals to use while experiencing a transitional moment. If used as stated, all crystals should assist in lightening a heaving load.

This chapter discusses three significant and relatable seasons of transition, so three of my favorite crystals within the same family were chosen here.

TRANSITIONING INTO PURPOSE

They have been personally identified as being highly effective in assisting with lightening the load. Black Calcite aids in regression and regaining memories so that the past can be released. The Clear Calcite is a stone of new beginnings. It acts as a detoxifier, cleansing and aligning all higher and lower chakras at the same time offering the gift of deep soul healing and revitalization of the subtle bodies. The Pink Calcite is a crystal that releases the fear and grief that keeps the heart trapped in the past, bringing in unconditional love. This stone of forgiveness aids in self-worth and self-acceptance, heals nervous conditions, lifts tension and anxiety overall making it a great benefit to someone who has suffered trauma or assault.

Maybe this is your first experience with crystals. Take your time and keep the faith.

God Is The Head Of My Life

God is the head of my life, that's all there is and that's the way it is. Alpha and Omega, the beginning and the ending of every situation and experience. Submission to thy will knowing that in God all things are possible. Knowing and believing that all sickness can be healed. Knowing and believing that it is in God and for God that we live and move and have our being. Never ending supply of everlasting love, my father, my mother, God, creator of Heaven and Earth is love and I am Made In His Image. I am the Spear of love in which all planets, All Stars, are beings, all creations reflect that love. I am the love that prevails the whole universe. I can perform all duties only after borrowing the power of action from God who is the first love of my life, the First Love Of My Heart, the first ambition of my soul, the first goal of my will, after putting God first in my life, I have the will and energy to do anything that I want to do, to become that higher self. All that is good, all there is. Divine mind in action because God is the head of my life, and we are one. ~The Spirit Within Colette (5/28/1986)

As we move forward, I want to share with you some of my own transitions. The first is losing my parents, then I speak candidly about saving my mental health, and finally, I discuss part of my spiritual awakening.

TRANSITIONING INTO PURPOSE

Transitions #1

LOSING MY PARENTS

Daddy died first. He was fearless all of his life, even in death. Just 5 years later, my Mama died. The situation was juxtaposed, as she was more frightened at the thought of death.

To witness the up-close experience as your parents transitioned from physical to spiritual form left me awestruck. Both of my parents were very audacious individuals who stood firm in what they believed. They were also both very vocal about their understanding of the spiritual realm. Although both Mama and Daddy frequently acknowledged and spoke highly of our ancestors, Daddy prepared me for his transition, yet Mama did not.

Imani Faith

After enduring some health challenges resulting in his being hospitalized leading up to his transition, Daddy made it quite clear to his children that he did not want to ever be resuscitated should it be questioned. Daddy always told us that he lived 7 lives so far, therefore he taught us very early that life is an eternity of living and resurrecting.

Having many conversations leading up to his death he expressed that he had made peace with his purpose while in physical form, at the same time made sure to provide a solid foundation for his children to follow. Overall, he was quite pleased with the impact that he had in his life. He was deeply entrenched in the community of conscious minded healthy eating individuals.

TRANSITIONING INTO PURPOSE

As I sat at Daddy's bedside, I held his right hand as I stared at the numbers on the respirator machine gradually dropping. Gratitude filled my mind and heart as I reflected on the fullness of who my Daddy was and how special it was that GOD chose him to be my father. I couldn't help but reflect on the many conversations we shared preparing me for the sadness in which I felt. At the same time there was a kind of peace that soon took precedence.

The numbers continued to drop, meanwhile I openly shared with him some of my future plans as it related to everything that he instilled in me. Minutes later, I looked over to my younger sister as she sobbed while holding his left hand. I glanced back at the respirator and then looked at Daddy's face.

It was then that I observed the process of the transition from the physical to spiritual for the first time in my life. Daddy slept peacefully taking one last breath and opening his mouth to release what seemed to be the longest exhale ever. Little did I know, as Daddy was undergoing his transition, I was embarking on one of my own. Daddy's was physical and mine more spiritual.

However, Mama's seemed to be completely different. Although she appeared to be very in tune with the spiritual realm, her ancestors, particularly her maternal and paternal ancestry, her acceptance of the afterlife were not intact. Mama still had some healing to do and quite a few goals she saw herself accomplishing before that time arrived.

TRANSITIONING INTO PURPOSE

Mama made it very clear through her words and actions that what looked challenging was only temporary. Mama also made sure to remind me how to embrace everything she is and was as her child. Mama taught me about awareness and the importance of family, while Daddy taught me the many aspects of laying the foundation as it relates to generational wealth creation. They both taught me the importance of loving myself and being mindful of what I consumed internally and externally. Although Daddy prepared me for his transition, no one would have thought 5 years and a few months later, that same preparation would be needed for Mama.

I know this seems illusory, but Mama's transition was beautiful, something I couldn't have ever imagined.

Imani Faith

Maybe it was because Mama was wide awake, and Daddy wasn't coherent. The day Mama died was a day not to be forgotten. Reflecting back, the day was so divine, as I recall my nephew turning her bed towards the window, so she would be able to get a glimpse of the sun as it rose and set. Then, my older sister made sure to bring something that would have her and her room smelling like she personally picked the flowers to create the most beautiful fragrance designed just for her. All the while, my older brother balanced it all by playing her favorite music that entire day.

Meanwhile, my plan was to restart her locks for her hair. She was awake and had previously inquired about me doing them in weeks past.

TRANSITIONING INTO PURPOSE

However, I really needed a nap but considering my sister had just left for the evening and my brother had gone to the car to take a short break, that was almost impossible. I wanted to keep an eye on Mama.

It was just Mama and me. Though she was unable to talk due to the significant amount of fluid in her lungs, this particular day she appeared to be more alert than any other day that she had been in the hospital. The process began with her looking around the room, particularly toward the ceiling and the window. I was on the couch while observing her and then I went to lie next to her as I was curious about what she was experiencing. As I laid there, her breathing became labored and the sound of the fluid that filled her lungs became louder.

Trying not to fear what was happening, while holding back the tears from the emotionality of it all, at that point I knew Mama was leaving me, leaving us.

In an instance, it became clearer that my job that day was to be there to calm her, as I calmed myself. My goal was to assist with making her outro as smooth as she made my introduction into this world. As I held her hand, I told her how much I admired her strength, her beauty, her endurance. I told her how I knew that our ancestors were in the room and although I couldn't honestly say that I was ready for them to take her with them, I knew that she would be happier with the transition. I continued to talk to her about following through with dreams in which she set forth for us by both.

TRANSITIONING INTO PURPOSE

As my body was close to hers, I could feel her heart take intervals of rest before resuming its normal rhythm. As I noticed the pattern of pauses then regularity, I decided to lay my head on her chest. A flow of tears followed each heartbeat.

However, I noticed that things slowly shifted from calm to movement. Her eyes widened, as foamed filled her mouth. A gurgling noise ensued as she moved her head side to side. Startled by it all, I called in a nurse. She confirmed that Mama had reached her final phase of death. Within five minutes the gurgling started to fade, the head movement ceased, and her eyes became relaxed. Eventually, her heart began to take on a rhythm of its own until it finally stopped forever.

Imani Faith

I was more in awe than scared. I had not done my research on death and dying, so the astonishment of what I had witnessed outweighed the fear that tried to creep in. How could I not be scared? How could I not be overwhelmed with sadness? How could I not think to immediately call my siblings? What was happening was well beyond my control. See, I had lived a life of attempting to control situations and outcomes, but that was a thing of the past. I had recently learned to make living in the moment a key priority. I was grateful to incorporate that lesson with Mama that day. But there was still an unanswered question.

Why me? I pondered on the thought well after Mama's transition. Why was I left in the room with Mama alone?

TRANSITIONING INTO PURPOSE

After discussing the sequence of events leading up to Mama's transition with my siblings, everyone admitted to not being able to handle such a responsibility. At the same time, we realized that everyone was comfortable in the role in which they played towards making Mama's transition as smooth as possible.

I now understand the alignment and significance of the preparation process. As I mentioned before, Daddy prepared me for transition, yet Mama did not. However, Mama always had a strong gift of attunement as it relates to her closely related ancestors. Not saying that Daddy did not have this gift as well, but Mama chose to share her many personal spiritual encounters and experiences particularly those that involved loved ones within the spirit realm more often than Daddy would.

Imani Faith

The strength that was endured through the brief emotional attack moments involving guilt, grief, isolation and loneliness was a direct result of time well spent during my parents preparation process. Without them knowing…it was ultimately both of my parents responsibility to train me how to keep the momentum of life's cycles going, by any means necessary. They both in their own unique way taught me how to cherish the past, embrace the present and how not to stop reaching for the future!

It's because of Mama that I am quite sensitive in knowing when her spirit and the spirits of our ancestors are around me; and it's because of Daddy that I am able to embrace each and every moment of transition knowing that transition is what paves the way towards purpose.

TRANSITIONING INTO PURPOSE

Purpose of Transition Statement: Betty Eadie said it like this, "*Life does not end when we die. Death is a rebirth into a spirit world of light and love, a transition from the spiritual that is no more frightening or painful than passing between rooms through an open doorway. It is a joyful homecoming to our natural home...*"

Healing

Father/Mother, God creator of Heaven and Earth You are ever present in all my being, you are my life. Energize my mind, body and soul. Let me feel by spirit. Help me to reject all negative forces in and about me. Restoring my mind and my body to perfect health and incline my heart to keep Thy Laws. Obedience to God's physical laws is the method to avoiding bodily ills. All in all, it's reaping what you sow, Cause and Effect, Karma. We make our own Happiness by obeying and disobeying God's Physical and Spiritual Laws.
~ The Spirit Within Colette

Transitions # 2

BECOMING HOSPITALIZED

That day I felt like dying. I recall being on the side of the road, minutes prior to that, I was driving while in heavy thought. It felt like an out-of-body experience of sorts. I was in conversation with God that day. I mentioned to Him that if this was the life that was chosen for me that I no longer wanted it. Crying hysterically, I imagined driving into oncoming traffic. Yet I was concerned, because I did not desire to hurt others in my process. So, I thought of another plan: "I'd drive into the lake on Lakeshore Drive." But then, I wanted it to be a more promising quick death.

I was in a battle. I knew something was wrong because I no longer recognized myself. It was the worst day of my life. I was terrified on the side of the road by myself with my own thoughts. Immediately, I knew this thing was much bigger than what I could handle alone. I called my sister. I needed help. That day my Mama and sister convinced me to check myself into the psychiatric ward of the same hospital in

TRANSITIONING INTO PURPOSE

which I was born. Here's snippets of what I recalled during that time:

> **Day 1: Pure Hell and Disbelief.** *I was put in a room with no tv and no windows, just me and my thoughts.*
>
> **Day 2: Observation and Reflection.** *I was in the room for 24-hours frustrated at the fact that I didn't have a window to jump out of.*
>
> *I was also perturbed at the fact that there was no food allowed. I decided to take a stroll to the community room. Obama was almost president that year. As I strolled down the hall, the news of it was all over the television screen and I could hear conversations of others around me.*
>
> *As I scanned the room, it became obvious this place was real and people there suffered from major mental illnesses and needed extreme assistance. My anxiety and feeling of an out-of-body experience only intensified. Immediately, the nurse came with the first round of medicine. I took it. I sat in the chair, the feelings of being lost*

and confused permeated all of me. At the same time, I felt traumatized by the reality of what was happening around me. Why was I there?

I remember questioning SELF, "What the hell is wrong with you girl?" "Are you seeking some type of attention?" "Are you going through some kind of midlife crisis?" Being that I ironically was able to check in and out of consciousness was when I realized that SELF was still present.

I'd had enough for that day and decided to go to bed in hopes of a better start tomorrow. As I journeyed back to my room, preparing myself for bed, my roommate came in to ask if I was okay.

The night before, she asked the same exact question, but I wasn't in a state of mind to answer or make eye contact with her.

It was my first night and I had experienced a roller coaster of emotions. I needed some real rest. So, I made eye contact and readied myself to respond.

TRANSITIONING INTO PURPOSE

As I stared at this lady, I looked deeper. Her face became familiar to me. She was my roommate, but also the mother of one of my former clients. The client and I developed a deep rapport while working together.

I grew to love her as my own child. I knew her story and knew it well. It was one of dysfunction, largely caused by her mother, my now roommate.

I wanted to respond about how I was doing, but memories of conversations about how she had abandoned and even disowned her own daughter flooded my mind. The memories of struggle and persistence of her daughter during some gruesome times, in hopes of continuing her education, were on constant replay. Motivational talks about her pushing through pain, was medicine I was taking for myself that day.

My roommate had been diagnosed with bipolar/schizophrenia disorder but had neglected to take her medication while trying to raise her child. After my client graduated from eight grade, this lady-her mom, failed to enroll her in high school.

Still, my client persisted through all of her trials, but now her mother, my now roommate, had been unable to be reached by her daughter for the last six months.

She wanted to know how I was doing but, as I looked at her face to face, I was glad to know she was good.

Day 3: Wake up Call. *So many emotions and thoughts ran through my mind. There were so many tasks for me to complete before the day ended. I had so much to accomplish.*

It was that day that I recognized that more of me was there than the adversary. I had no desire to join in with the community and eating was not my concern. I stayed in my room the majority of the time. My mom had managed to slip some positive books in my bag for reading. Reading, along with a few naps in between, had become my mode of operation.

TRANSITIONING INTO PURPOSE

I tried to uncover ways to connect with my roommate without her discovering who I was. The task was difficult. Why was I there? Was it just to locate my client's mom for her? I'm not sure.

Towards the end of the day, I realized that although we may not understand the why, what and when of every situation, everything indeed happens for a particular reason.

The teacher had become the client and student. I was learning and embracing this shift, this new transition.

Therefore, if I truly desired to gain clarity and direction, the time had come to finally give into SELF. To allow transition to take place.

Day 4: The Meeting and Self-Identity. *My family came. All of them sat at the table, all of them. My was ex-husband there, also my current mate was present, my mother, along with the social worker were there as well.*

Imani Faith

They also strategized to create an aftercare plan for me. The plan was supposed to 'fix me' coupled with the medicines they would select with the aid of the psychiatrist. I sat there and observed it all, but I couldn't help but feel more claustrophobic than safe.

Although the people at the table, including my loved ones, were supposed to come together to construct a plan of support, I wasn't convinced that I wouldn't be alone.

After all, they each were a part of the reason I had landed in the psychiatric ward in the first place.

I couldn't wait for them to leave. In an ideal circumstance, their presence would have initiated relief. However, being there was like an escape from them. The pressure I felt from them was all too much.

Everything else that occurred in between, was a blur. Finally, I said my goodbyes, faked my medicine dosage and hurried back to my room. I needed a different connection. It was then that I realized that SELF was a direct connection to

TRANSITIONING INTO PURPOSE

GOD. I define SELF as being one with the pure form of GOD's creation, made purposefully in his image and likeness. The more I talked to GOD the more SELF appeared in the psychiatric ward. The more I motivated, encouraged, and spoke life to SELF, the more GOD spoke back, providing me with necessary tools making it possible to understand my purpose at that moment.

It was then that I began to examine my SELF identity. It was then that I made the choice to purposefully live for SELF and not others. It was then that I knew that being in the hospital was beyond what the naked eye could see and was designed to be my moment of stillness. This was a major transition.

"Ok God I get it", I tell myself. So now that I'm back, I have 24 hours to reunite the woman who sleeps in the bed next to me with her family. Immediately, I clearly heard , 'write her a letter and leave it on her pillow tomorrow once you're discharged.' So that's exactly what I did.

Imani Faith

Day 5: Clarity and Testimony. *For the first time waking up in that room felt more like the end of a conquered task rather than that of intense trauma. It was like for the first time in days, I looked forward to the outcome of the day rather than how fast the day would end.*

As I sat on the side of the bed to reflect on my experience, clarity set in.

That day, I gained full clarity when it came to the endurance, strength, determination and obedience that God instilled in me.

I also recognized that as traumatic as this experience may have been, I needed to go through it so that I would be a walking testimony for others not knowing when they may simply need a moment of stillness in order to elevate to their highest potential. God took me to the psychiatric ward for that transitional period. For that, I'm grateful.

TRANSITIONING INTO PURPOSE

In conclusion, not only did I connect with SELF in preparation for more life changing events, but my roommate successfully reunited with her daughter approximately a week after my discharge. Little did I know that SELF was just getting started.

God Is

God is a very intelligent Spirit or Force. God is the master of all life. God is I am that I am. God is Jehovah. God is Allah. God is Elohim. God is Yahweh. God is Rah. God is positive thought and action. God is peace. God is love. God is discipline. My God Is Heaven within, and Above. God is time. God is being in Harmony with all life. God is breath. God is that change, called death. God is that peace within that says breathe deep, think deep. Know that he's with you, even in your sleep. God is the Inhalation and Exhalation of all life. God is faith. God is that will, to do all good things. God is truth. My God is that all seeing eye for justice. And equality. My God is forgiving. My God is kindness. My God is understanding. My God is he and he is us and we are he.. My God can also be like a rose, so sweet, exotic peace, so beautiful.
~The Spirit Within Colette

Imani Faith

Life After Being Discharged...

There was so much more work that God had planned for me and the fight was real every step of the way. There were times that being obedient came naturally and there were many times I questioned what I knew needed to be done. Was I ready to share with the world that I had been admitted and released from the psych ward?

Did I want to put in the work to remove myself from all which was toxicity around me? Could I handle standing up to my mother who was a strong force in all decisions that I've ever made? She had subconsciously had a spirit of control over me. Was I ready to let go of my fear, pride, control and idle ways in order for God to truly use me? Absolutely not! I wasn't ready for any of it. However, deep down I knew the only way to reach my full potential was to GET READY cause this was just the beginning!

> **Purpose of Transition Statement:** *"When we focus on clarifying what is being observed, felt, and needed rather than on diagnosing and judging, we discover the death of our own compassion."*
> *- Marshall B*

Transition #3

WHAT'S THIS CHURCH THING ALL ABOUT?

Many days I've found it to be a struggle living in two spiritual worlds. I can recall the exact moment of disconnect while attending church. That morning I woke up yearning to be fed spiritually. However, once I made it to the church, the announcement of there being a guest speaker, loomed in my mind with disappointment. The pastor chose to attend the NBA All-Star game instead of nourishing the parishioners.

Considering the ongoing problem with absenteeism, I was enraged with frustration. It was not my first encounter with being dissatisfied, it was just my last.

On the way home, I decided to turn on the gospel radio station. That day became life altering day for me. The pastor on the radio began teaching from the book of Ruth. Though far in the distant past, I automatically recalled the sermon from that day.

The sermon focused on *7 Significant Steps for Your Life*...below are some notes I was able to capture that I want to share with you:

TRANSITIONING INTO PURPOSE

1. You must know what you are going after. *You must have a specific target in mind.* Deuteronomy 5:21; Romans 8:28.

2. *Wash your face.* Don't let your past affect your future. You can't move forward until you wash your face off, or you will forfeit your future.

3. *Anoint your face.* Put on a fresh, positive attitude. Serve the Lord with gladness. Philippians 3:14

4. *Change your garments.* Prepare for where you are going. A prepared person is prepared for something that hasn't happened. Be ready. Now is the season to remove distractions out of the way. Meditate on what God said. Look ahead.

5. *Get down to the floor.* Get to the place that the blessing will come from. It

Imani Faith

doesn't matter where you start, it matters where you'll finish.

6. *When you get into place, shut your mouth.* Get into place and wait. Just wait. They that wait on the Lord shall renew their strength.

7. *Don't try to shine when the light is not on you.* Write down a goal and plan for the goal.

It was then that I understood the statement by Abraham Hicks, *"You can meet your inner being in church, but you don't have to go to church to meet your inner being."* Don't be confused, the church is the majority of what I knew but it wasn't the full extent of what I was exposed to.

My experience was sort of complexed. Imagine growing up in a household in which

TRANSITIONING INTO PURPOSE

your mother catches what was identified as the "Holy Ghost" occasionally on a Sunday morning after marching in with a choir singing how much she loves Jesus. Then, to come home to your dad sarcastically ask how it was serving y'all white Jesus?! That was my daily experience. Not only was it a norm to celebrate the birth and life of Jesus Christ, but my mother was very involved in the church. However, she referred to him as Yahshua. Her father exposed the family to the Black Hebrew Israelites under the leadership of Yahweh Ben Yahweh at the time. It gets deeper.

There was a portion of time that my immediate family lived by the belief system of Christianity and Judaism at the forefront. We were also exposed to Islam, Buddhist, Coptic Faith and Yoruba practices as well. My maternal great grandmother also was very profound in my family's lives and was the minister of her own spiritualist church in which prophetic words were given frequently.

As I grew older, I learned that there was one commonality--I AM was present in each practice. The questions still persisted--who was God exactly? And how can I tell which one was most beneficial for me? How would I reach him and know it?

Finally reaching the age to make my own decision when it came to religion, I still ran into profound issues. I felt utterly powerless and disconnected. Shortly after leaving the church in which my mom raised me, I became heavily involved in a Pentecostal church movement. Once I went off to college, I had to deal with my first teenage pregnancy and soon came back home pregnant with my second child. Both I and my children's father were raised in church.

So, as we were building our family, we attended a Pentecostal church. However, shortly after our arrival, we were told that in order to remain in the church we first needed to be married immediately. We were instructed that God was displeased with us and the only way to make it right was to repent and be married immediately. My children's father agreed with the church's leadership, but I did not. I had a decision to make---raise the children in a one-parent home or go with the premature marriage plan.

I chose the latter. I was unhappy from the start. I felt as if I had signed my entire life over to a church. My life had become church. I began feeling that every action I took was under the microscope. My then husband was led under the churches' leadership. Everything he was instructed to do, was done.

Decisions about our household were made with involvement from the church and not me.

However, my fiasco with the church was far from done. I had countless judgmental church leaders call and rebuke me. There were constant actions that were suspect on my part. Some children were told to speak in tongues and follow suit. A countless number of members were intentionally knocked out and was told that it was by the spirit. There were instances that individuals were called out for stealing funds from the church. Sometimes, less fortunate families were manipulated to sow large financial seeds. I do admit, however, despite all of this, there were several times when the presence of God was evident.

However, there were times the feeling of a demonic presence circulated and surfaced as well. As I attended the services, my body became physically drained. Overall, I experienced many positive attributes and had significant lessons learned while attending the church.

However, those experiences did not overshadow the uncanniness of it all! After removing myself from what clearly felt like a cult, I was traumatized by it and found myself disappointed in what the church had become. As time passed, I found myself craving the desire of worship in the house of God once again. Although I prayed regularly and recognized God to be the head of my life, it still

Imani Faith

wasn't clear that the relationship had actually been established. I realized that I settled some.

There were encounters for me to experience, but it was a time where true revelation needed to take place. I was back seeking and scouting out different churches hoping to find that one!

After following my mother for a short time and frequently visiting churches in which she was invited, I was led to the previous church mentioned (I avoid the name to protect the entity). At the start, it was everything I ever wanted. From the fulfillment of morning worship, bible study for myself and the children, and a church choir that reminded me of my childhood. It was incredible. Also, the pastor was led by God. I regained my motivation and started attending religiously. Then, increasingly, the pastor started to skip out on services.

For the first couple of months, although I was disappointed a bit, I didn't complain and was consistent with attendance. Soon, the ministers were evidently attention seeking instead of spiritually mature. I had some decisions to make and quick.

The Pastor had frequently missed service due to his attendance at celebrity events and had on a few occasions interrupted the flow of service because he didn't want people to exit the service during offering periods. Once, he actually instructed the ushers to block the doors. It was all a bit baffling for me. The commercialization of church services has been a turn off for me and in my experience, lacked a deep spiritual element.

Imani Faith

Caveat, there are many powerful Christian leaders that I still support and follow online. I even visit their church from time to time. However, there is no strong desire to commit to following one spiritual leader other than the GOD that lives within SELF.

In all, though I've had these outrageous experiences, I have not totally given up on the church. However, I have yet to find the one that best suits my holistic needs. Until then, I have continued to have church within SELF. Now more than ever, I understand that the guidance outside me could never replace guidance inside of me.

Purpose of Transition Statement: *Romans 12:2- Do not conform to the pattern of this world but be transformed by the renewing of your mind.*

TRANSITIONING INTO PURPOSE

To Be In The World, But Not Of It

There are many spirits in this land
It is the land of Good and Plenty.
You must be strong, or you won't last long.
It's all up to you.
Sometimes when you're feeling a little blue because you've been met with a challenge or two,
Give yourself a kiss from (YOU) and then turn within and give yourself a kiss from me too.
I'm there, right inside of you. I am the genius who's in Jesus within (YOU)
Now take a deep breath.
I'm there!
I'm even in the air.
I am the one and only Spirit that's fair.
I come alive as you read, as you sing praises unto thee
I am the thought that you think constructively.
I am the spirit of the Lord thy God Within Thee.
~The Spirit Within Colette
Copyright 1983

Life After Church

Now that I have gained a level of clarity on who I am in relation to God, I want to reflect on some

Imani Faith

key moment in my life beyond church. Experience is indeed the best teacher.

When I consider wholeheartedly my mother's connection to my childhood church, I remain truly grateful.

To have been raised under such incredible leaders, Bishop Andrew Gooden and Reverend Ernest Charles Bell, had an immeasurable impact on my life. The more I learned about what was needed for my spiritual and emotional well-being, the more I am reminded as to where it first originated--my childhood church.

The power of affirmations, colors, numbers, candle burning, being in alignment, the freedom to love, forgiveness, imperfections, change in seasons, sowing seeds, infinite intelligence and how it all is connected to the bible is where my foundation lies.

TRANSITIONING INTO PURPOSE

There you have it. My mother found a church home that resonated with almost everything in which she stood for spiritually. All she had to do was ask and be ready to receive and so she did just that!

Not even realizing that my decision to follow *The Spirit Within* would be cultivated in such a way, travelling throughout my legacy then transformed to be something greater than I could have ever imagined according to God's plan!!

Imani Faith

FAITH IS

Peaceful Practice

The subconscious law of success is to repeat affirmations, prayers, and statements to yourself daily. You must take this time for yourself. There's time for everything. Say affirmations or statements with deep feelings with intense concentration. Recite them at the beginning of your day, at noonday, and say them as you are going to sleep. Don't doubt and castaway the thought of failure because you are a child of God. Believe that you are an heir to all of God's goodness and wealth. Start now. Write down some of your own affirmations that you can begin to speak to yourself daily.

_____

_____

_____

_____

_____

_____

_____

_____

_____

TRANSITIONING INTO PURPOSE

SECTION TWO

What is a Solstice and Equinox?

Solstice means "the standing of the sun or the sun stands still." There are two solstices that occur per year, winter and summer. This happens when northern and southern hemispheres receive different amounts of sunlight. The winter solstice occurs on the first day of the winter, which represents its start.

Imani Faith

It is described to be the shortest day of the year and has the smallest amount of daylight. It also marks when the earth is tilted farthest away from the sun, which is what causes temperatures in the northern hemisphere to start to decrease.

Then there is summer solstice which occurs on the first day of summer, which is described to be the longest day of the year and longest amount of sunlight. It's not until the Earth starts tilting back towards the sun after the spring equinox that the temperature will start to increase again representing the start of summer. These transitions are happening while we are mostly unaware. They represent living, dying and restarting, therefore gaining and identifying clarity as it relates to our existence here on Earth.

TRANSITIONING INTO PURPOSE

An equinox is a point in the year when daytime and nighttime are exactly the same length, 24 hours each. Equinoxes occur twice a year usually in March, representing the start of spring and in September representing the start of fall. This happens when the earth is tilted neither towards nor away from the Sun. The equinoxes and solstices are caused by Earth's tilt on its axis and ceaseless motion in orbit.

In the northern hemisphere, the March equinox will bring earlier sunrises, late sunsets, softer winds, and sprouting plants. Meanwhile south of the equator you'll find in the opposite season. There will be later sunrises, earlier sunsets, chillier winds, and dry and falling leaves. You might ask, how does the solstices and equinox lessons relate to the chapters going forward? I'm so glad you asked.

Imani Faith

It's understood that the Earth is constantly in rotation according to the geography of the solstice and equinox. Spiritually, one can relate it to balance (equal) and seasonal change (solstice). Not only is it a time of earthly seasonal change, I understand and identify these as a time of self-change. Each solstice and equinox period mentioned going forward represents a season in which a new spiritual, transitional period takes place for the author.

Furthermore, solstice and equinox are a constant reminder of the journey travelled. Just like the moon and the sun, cycling through seasons, we ourselves go through similar patterns of luminescence, energy and then release. Throughout history, while people have long gathered around the world to celebrate and honor the movement of the Sun through special rituals, simple gatherings, dance and

TRANSITIONING INTO PURPOSE

ceremonies, I understand it as a time of reflection. Solstice and equinox seasonal change is also used as a way to celebrate my unique journey and the inheritance cycles within walking spiritual paths and living a human life as well. This has become my natural way to reconnect with life's divine plan and to feel a deep connection to all of life and the natural world.

Imani Faith

TRANSITIONING INTO PURPOSE

Start of Winter Solstice: New Transition Phase

Purgings Renewals ⇆Intentions

2
RESURRECTION TIME[2]

You don't have to be great to get started but you have to get started to be great! -Les Brown

THINGS TO CONSIDER:

Challenge Question: What or who must I release in order to embrace change?

Affirmation: *The most powerful thing I can do is love myself (inspired by Louise Hay)*

Healing Crystal: Rainbow Moonstone

LOUISE HAYS 10 RULES FOR SUCCESS:

love yourself
be mindful of your words
don't be resentful
learn how to think successfully
help others
be calm
do affirmations

---

[2] Inspired by: Yahshua Ben Israel and Louise Hay

Imani Faith

keep working on yourself
be thankful
believe that only good lies ahead

As I reflected on the various moments and seasons of transition, which can also be identified as moments of elevation, I began to understand the correlation of my Daddy's poem "COME ALIVE RESURRECTION TIME." What I witnessed thus far, were moments of physical change and positive growth aiding in the rebirth of something far greater than what was imagined. I now understand that when something is put to rest, it dies, momentum has stopped, and source is no longer supplying an energy flow. Just as something slows down and dies or goes through transition, momentum gives opportunity to procreate, therefore preparing for something fresh and new to come to life!

TRANSITIONING INTO PURPOSE

Shortly after coming home from the hospital was when I experienced resurrection for the first time, I felt an out-of-body experience.

To which, I will never forget. The moment of rebirth was now alive and in full effect as I intentionally shout out affirmations of gratitude while giving praise to the Most High. I recognized as "I Am that I Am, creator of Heaven and Earth", this was done through acts of song and dance while listening to my favorite gospel music. I vividly recall the intensity of vibration that traveled through my body during those moments. It was like all that weighed me down had been released. It was like I was at the start of a race preparing for take-off, not concerning myself with the challenges and obstacles that I may face while traveling towards the finish line.

Not because I didn't care, but because the excitement and gratitude in which I felt to even be chosen to run the race is what took precedence. So, the more I lifted my voice in praise, the more momentum geared towards new life. Now that resurrection had taken place and it had been identified that I was ALIVE, what was next? Next, it was time to shift my mindset. I specifically focused on learning the difference between what was, what is and what will be. Furthermore, accepting the past, embracing the present and believing that the best is yet to come was another mindset shift!

TRANSITIONING INTO PURPOSE

Girl, It Will Grow Back

"It's just hair," I said, as I watched the sadness in Mama's eyes. Mama had a strong connection to her locks and was not ready to let them go. Although she knew that they were dying one by one judging by the number of detached locks that she had collected thus far, Mama did not want to accept the reality that she might have to let them go by cutting her hair off. The pruning would give her hair a break for a while and then starting over once her hair became strong enough again.

This is another example of transition and a perfect example of how the healing process works while going through a rebirthing experience.

Imani Faith

Although we may not understand or want to, sometimes we have to let things go or die off in order to allow new life to produce. It's times like this when more spiritual grounding may be needed in order to truly accept the current emotions by making it a part of the present, furthermore, using the present emotion as motivation while gearing up for what's to come.

Meanwhile, I left Mama that day, only to return with a half sided shaved head. Mama couldn't believe what she saw when she looked at me. 'Why would you do that to all of your beautiful hair?" I said, again with confidence, "it's just hair, it'll grow back, for I needed a change anyway". With a bit of sarcasm, I said, "change is good for the soul. Wouldn't you like to try it out?" Mama smiled.

TRANSITIONING INTO PURPOSE

Let's get a bit more personal. What about you? What or who in your life no longer serves a purpose that you are ready to release?

I know, that came out of nowhere. However, I want you to identify areas in your own life that need some attention. What are some things and people you can release to help your greater good? What has prevented you in making change happen? What steps can you take to make a change **today**?

Once you answer those questions a real transition can take place. Now is it time to focus on renewals (what is) and then intentions (what will be).

Imani Faith

The Power of Affirmations

Mama always expressed the importance of what one allows to come out of their mouth and the significance in the power of the tongue. However, I would never have imagined that the same resources which she used to assist and aid in a healing process, would be the same resources needed as a reminder to what I knew to be true and highly effective.

So how do we really embrace and cope with reality although it may not appear to look or feel good?

We focus on the feeling of what we want, then we begin to speak that of what we want, therefore manifesting what we want.

It's a process.

TRANSITIONING INTO PURPOSE

Eventually there came a point while being in that hospital room with nowhere to go and no one to talk to that my thoughts and feelings were all I was left with. It was author Louise Hayses work, that I depended on to get me to the next level. As I came across one of the books my Mama put in my bag, Hays said, "You can heal your life," I was empowered. This was a game changer for me. I took it in an made it a part of me.

The more I read the more at peace I became. The more intentional I became while reading, the more focused I became on the word itself. The more I believed in the power of the words I continued to recite, the more perfect, whole and complete I felt.

Transition Activated, Resurrection is Now Alive!

Imani Faith

I choose the Rainbow Moonstone here because it is a stone of new beginnings; it's used to help face life's changing decisions as well as teaches one to view what may appear to be a stressful ending as a positive process. The stone is said to be encouraging of rest and relaxation periods in order to see the beauty that lies ahead. Tip: Hold the moonstone in hand while visualizing what you want to manifest.

Purpose of Transition Statement: I aim to reduce all needless pressure in my life. "All the suffering, stress and addiction comes from not realizing you are already what you are looking for"-Jon Kab

Thank You God for a New Awakening

I thank you God For A New Awakening ...If any man be in Christ, he is a new creature; old things are passed away; behold, all things become new.~ 2 Corinthians 5:17 Have you heard a saying, "I'm not what I want to be but I'm not what I used to be?" Using certain principles help us grow and go in the direction of our desires. Happiness is the one thing we all desire. When we consciously connect to God, we awaken within ourselves the realization that thoughts are things and therefore we choose our thoughts more selectively and good changes occur because of the choices we make. We cannot see the results right away, even though they are there, similar to the caterpillar that turns into a beautiful butterfly! Good thoughts attract good reactions. It is the happiness we desire, that compels us to see change in order to be what we want to be. It is wonderful to know that just by changing the way we think, we will never be the same again. We must be aware of our thoughts at all times. ~The Spirit With Colette

TRANSITIONING INTO PURPOSE

FAITH IS

Peaceful Practice

To recover, one has to look within themselves. There are a lot of beautiful things in there. Love, great peace, and great power within the Lord thy God. Reject all negative forces in and around you. Ask this great unseen healing force to restore you to perfect health starting now. Write down things you can speak to create peace in and around you. Record them below.

_____

_____

_____

_____

_____

_____

_____

_____

_____

_____

_____

_____

_____

_____

_____

Imani Faith

3
Divine Infinite Intelligence/Mind Control[3]

Life is a balance stop holding on and letting go -Rumi

THINGS TO CONSIDER:

Challenge Question: In what ways do you aim to reduce unnecessary pressure that you encounter? Write down your answers.

Affirmation: *I am blessed with infinite intelligence; I reject any negative force in and about me.* (Inspired by Rev. Bell)

Healing Crystal: Green Fluorite and Amethyst

The time has come to focus on the solution. This is a time where you will practice remaining stable in an unstable environment. Get this... energy flows where attraction goes.

---

[3] Inspired by Abraham Hicks and Rev. Ernest C. Bell (childhood pastor)

Imani Faith

You don't have to create energy, you have an infinite amount, just let it flow.

The more I found myself in a space of disbelief with thoughts that led to what appeared to be uncontrolled actions, the more I knew that understanding and mastering divine infinite intelligence would require more work than intentionally control of the mind. One day, as I looked at myself in the mirror wanting to escape the emotional pain that I was feeling, it was then that I remembered that I was made in God's image and likeness; therefore, what was true about God had to be true about me. So, what did that mean for me? Considering God is the creator and originator of all that flows in and about, the intention should be to think and move Godlike at all times.

TRANSITIONING INTO PURPOSE

Now, to think Godlike was far from a walk in the park, however it became easier to recognize and then control misplaced emotional anger within self. I now understand that this newly identified power within myself is just awaiting to be cultivated. So, as I reflect on continued new beginnings and cultivating my own power as it relates to self-awareness, a spiritual tug of war and the choices made as an outcome, upholding and maintaining relationships come to mind.

Toxic Relationships

Know that God has provided a way of escape from any negative situation. You can't attract something unwanted without holding the vibration of that thing, entity or being.

Imani Faith

It is important to remain careful when it comes to the vibration of expectation of people.

Vibration is sometimes mixed with your last experiences. Vibration is a thought that is believed. A belief is a vibration that you continue to think. Expectations and beliefs are practiced thoughts. Avoid disappointments as a result of trying to be in control. You must change your thoughts. The ball is in your court. If you're in a toxic relationship, and choose to not remove yourself for whatever reason, make the best of it.

Stay true to yourself at all costs. You can't change someone, but you can change yourself and how you respond. You can also control how you respond to action done against you. You are not responsible for how someone else feels.

TRANSITIONING INTO PURPOSE

Believe it or not, we are natural harmonizers, stabilizers, and balancers. So often do we find ourselves in situations where we are trying to compensate; not even recognizing that attraction is a two-way street.

However, though there is a two-way street, understand that whatever or whoever is dominant will always have the control. In spite of what it can sometimes feel like, know that you are the creator of your own experience. This control in creating gets better with practice. It is important to practice thoughts that feel good. Divine infinite intelligence gives you an opportunity to define who you are and what you really want.

Make a decision and line up with it. Focus on you. This is the perfect time to isolate yourself from the naysayers if you need to.

Imani Faith

The ultimate plan must be to get to the point where you do not have to isolate in order to not focus on unwanted things.

Ultimately, the purpose of this section is to remind you of the satisfaction factor. Relationships though sometimes intricate, are supposed to feel good. Evolving and expanding is supposed to be rewarding. Think about it. When you cannot witness your growth, you are missing an incredible opportunity. There's a feeling of elation when you finally achieve a level of growth once aspired.

Divine Infinite Intelligence is a source, which is also identified as spirit. Spirit says, now that you have learned how to navigate negative emotions you can control what happens inside of you. You begin to focus on the direction of that new desire.

TRANSITIONING INTO PURPOSE

Therefore, you begin to experience the reception of knowledge, information and impulses, assisting you to move forward in ways you have been holding back. You find pure divine infinite excitement...now that's Divine Infinite Intelligence! As we wrap up in this section, I want to leave you with a few takeaways.

As for the healing stone chosen, I wanted to elaborate here. Green Fluorite is good for focus and concentration. Amethyst is that which connects with intellect and intellectual capacity. Green Fluorite is a harmonizing crystal. It inspires new ideas, originality and quick thinking. It aids in making sure that one's thoughts, words, and actions are aligned with their true purpose. The Amethyst is a stone tied to royalty, intuition, higher intelligence, spirituality, and divine love.

Imani Faith

It is supportive of one's spiritual awakening journey. Both crystals aid in manifesting the highest aspect of the mind which is attunement to Spirit and accessing one's intuitive powers. Both crystals can be used in meditation by holding in the palm of hand or placed in a sacred space.

Purpose of Transition Statement: In all, my goal was to develop spiritual stamina so that when a problem occurred, I would not react out of emotion, but instead out of wisdom. I hope the same for you. Your affirmation: **I will react out of wisdom instead of emotion.**

Captain Of The Ship

The captain of the ship sails to the port of many seas. The Sea of kindness, the Sea of Oneness, the Sea of self-awareness, the Sea of understanding, the Sea of Divine Love, the Sea of Peace, the Sea of Truth, The Sea of Godly love, the Sea of Brotherly and sisterly love. You know, the kind that everybody can see and Feel, The kind that makes you feel that, you're being healed all over... Navigators of our life that's what we are, we construct the path. How? By seeing Love, Peace, Health, Wealth, sharing and caring through our Mind's Eye. Whatever you choose to see. Because, what you see is what you get. We are the captains of many ships. We Are The Navigators of Our Fate, remember, what you see and what you say is what you get. Navigate, Construct, Create. Sail on Captain of the ship of many Ports. Up with the flag of Peace. Up with the flag of Brotherly and Sisterly Love. Up with the flag of Health. Up with the flag of Wealth. Sail on up the Sea of life with me my love, let's be Master Navigators. We have lots of help you know. Who? The God within me and the God within you.
Sail on Captain's, sail on.
~The Spirit Within Colette

TRANSITIONING INTO PURPOSE

FAITH IS

Peaceful Practice

Cultivate a peaceful attitude of mind. It is easier said than done, I know. It takes practice. Start by uprooting and disturbing all negative thought patterns. Plant the seed of love and joy. Let love and happiness grow. Think on something you thought negative today and write examples of ways you could replace those thoughts with something positive. Be honest. Jot down those examples below.

_____

_____

_____

_____

_____

_____

_____

_____

_____

_____

_____

_____

Imani Faith

TRANSITIONING INTO PURPOSE

Start of Spring Equinox: New Transition Phase

Plant the seeds⇆ Attract ⇆Motivate

4
Planting Seeds[4]

Keep planting new seeds until your mind becomes the earth that gives birth to new worlds.- Curtis Tyrone Jones

---

THINGS TO CONSIDER:

Challenge Question: How do I turn my thoughts into things? Am I what I attract/think? On a separate sheet of paper, write what you feel.

Affirmation: I am God's instrument of creation, so my responsibility is to create continually.

Healing Crystal: Tiger's Eye

I came to a point in my life where I had to realize personal responsibility. It was time for me to become responsible for things I thought and spoke. But how must one do that?

---

[4] **Inspired by:** Abraham Hicks and Dr. Moira Foxe

Though it appears to be a complicated question, spirit says, it's quite simple! The key was to become intentional about using and tapping into something that we are all gifted with at birth. It was at that moment that I developed a greater awareness of consciousness. "Wow," I thought. Everything is consciousness and I mean EVERYTHING is consciousness. I further realized that consciousness is derived from our mind and thoughts working together when it comes to every move that is made. Consciousness is basically the creative gift we were born with that allows us to focus with intent; therefore, there is no consciousness without perception. The practice is simple that you must pay attention to what happens and how you feel when it happens.

TRANSITIONING INTO PURPOSE

You cannot exist without coming to new desires however, new desire summons new energy. So, be sure to check it out. Just because you are summoned, doesn't mean you're in the receptive mode of letting new energy in.

Now how does consciousness relate to the seeds which are sown?

When a seed is planted, we don't truly know what the outcome of that plant will be. However, it is believed that it will grow into something beautiful or similar to what its imagined to be if time is invested to cultivate it, by watering it, giving it attention, and providing the right amount of sunlight. All we know is that it feels good to live in that moment. It becomes exciting to watch what will happen, once it's time to expect a harvest.

This is when I made peace with the art of 'allowing'. There is a continuous cycle of becoming that everyone is born with it.

Consciously, I found myself planting seeds but not taking the time to invest and cultivate the seed that has been planted. For some odd reason I believed that I could plant a seed and then leave it to fend for itself. Furthermore, I expected for it to sprout, however when growth is interrupted or if I did not physically see the outcome that was expected, disappointment and aggravation sat in. This then turned into a seed that was no longer active.

Now, I find it to be okay to reset in the present! The time had come to release the aggravated feeling of making my negative thoughts a part of my reality.

TRANSITIONING INTO PURPOSE

I choose to never again consciously and deliberately let go of what I started to create. This was especially true when I came to the point of being able to realize what was/is being created could potentially be beneficial for me as well as the greater good. I finally understood that the time came to create thoughts that would attract only the most beautiful things imagined. The time had come to be the action underneath the idea and find myself embodied with the idea, being one with it, therefore claiming it. This is consciousness.

I then made an effort to positively use, support and work the one mind I have as a result of consciousness, by finally owning it! This revelation has been enlightening and delightful because of the possibility in which it provides.

Imani Faith

So instead of thinking I had been victimized or limited, I regrouped and regained the power within. I gave this thing called consciousness a fair chance, by reclaiming, reusing and by making what my original idea was a *reality*.

I consciously choose to support the law of consciousness because I understand that if I work the law, the law will work for me. Then it will work through me, impacting the lives of those around me. Ultimately, the whole of life will be affected because the whole of life will be raised as a consequence of me and you raising our level of consciousness.

Blended Consciousness happens when you are intentionally aware of the consciousness of your inner being and vibrational wavelength.

TRANSITIONING INTO PURPOSE

This persists as the conscious of your inner being shares the same frequency and momentum of the consciousness of your outer being. You become fully aware and begin to manifest the reality that exists in all of the universe best creation (Abraham Hicks).

The key is to focus more on the seed that's being planted than on the harvest. Live in the moment of manifestation. Trust where you're going and have fun with it. Here are a few things to consider as you are watering seeds as you are becoming.

The Tiger's Eye stone chosen represents vitality and physical action. It is a unique stone known for building courage in all aspects of one's life. It challenges you to explore the unknowns of life, even if it gets uncomfortable.

Imani Faith

Its properties include transformation of one's perspective and also pushes you to move past any boundaries you have set for yourself. This crystal should be worn and carried in any environment to promote courage or a courageous outlook on life. Surround yourself with its empowering, motivating confidence-boosting properties and align yourself with its bold and courageousness characteristics by choosing to carry it , wear it or by placing it in an environment nearby. By doing so, you can tap into its energy whenever you need it.

Purpose of Transition Statement: The root of confidence is courage, it's important that we constantly remind ourselves that truth. We are spirit and our spirits do what they were designed to do, flow.

TRANSITIONING INTO PURPOSE

Build On It

"Being confident of this very thing that he hath begun a good work in you"
-Philippians 1:6

Be still and listen to God within, realize that you are blessed with directions and health warnings all within. We must build our confidence in knowing who we are and who's we are. We are born with infinite intelligence and with power beyond our understanding. God has equipped us with all we need, we just have to build upon it. When the mind is not on assignment give it a job to work for you. It would do what you tell it to. Tell it that no matter what the appearance or challenge, nothing and nobody shall disturb your peace. Build on good relationships with family, friends, work colleagues and community. There is nothing we can't do if we really want to. Continue to build on all those good things within and make sure you keep on the whole armor of God in case you run into a stumbling block. Let's be Builders of all good constructive things.

~The Spirit Within Colette Grant

Imani Faith

FAITH IS

Peaceful Practice

Happiness is an art you have to work towards. Like a job, you must work to reap the harvest thereof. Consider below, ways you can cultivate your own field of happiness. What practices could you put in place to ensure your own happiness daily?

_____
_____
_____
_____
_____
_____
_____
_____
_____
_____
_____
_____
_____
_____
_____
_____
_____

5
Everything Always Works Out For Me[5]

The Intuitive mind is a sacred gift; The rational mind is a faithful servant
~ Einstein

THINGS TO CONSIDER:

Challenge Question: Now that I know things always work out for me, what exactly do I want to work for me at the present moment?

Affirmation: I am in control of any and everything that has to do with my body and emotions.

Healing Crystal: Labradorite

The book "The Secret" was popular in 2006 in the metaphysical world. Typically, I move in opposition to the crowd. The talk of a movie soon followed and eventually, I succumbed to the pressure of this movement.

---

[5] Inspired by Abraham Hicks

Imani Faith

Once uncovering the thoughts behind the movement, it is an already embodied principle. For so long, I had believed in the art of manifestation and knew I had been working on and studying consciousness.

I discovered that your subconscious mind cannot differentiate between what's real and what's imagined. Whatever you impress, whether it is imagined, you hear it, you read it, or are emotionally involved with it, it is real in your world. This is what controls the vibration you are in. The vibration you are in is the frequency in which you are operating on. The desire alters the vibration, the vibration changes the action, the action sets up an attraction, and that is what changes the result. You have the ability to manifest what you are, not what you want. Be clear about what you want.

TRANSITIONING INTO PURPOSE

Take time and really explore your desire, then commit yourself to what you really care about. Your thoughts continuously flow freely towards what you want, after which, making it happen will naturally follow. Once you're able to maintain a steady stream of thought without changing direction, it will manifest as a reality in your life. Have faith, patience and engage in consistent action. Practice thoughts that feel good, the purpose of creation, then launch an alignment for the exhilaration that it brings.

Think about what it feels like to be drained after having a fun-filled, productive day. For most of us it is usually a high feeling of being on top of the world until we decide it's time to come down from it. Then think about what it feels like to be drained after having a day full of unwanted behaviors and intentions. Would you rather feel high from a good vibration or from a bad vibration? Everything is energy. Everything that will ever exist is already here in one form or another. Any life you want, you can attract. Make it your reality by getting into that frequency. Being receptive of the fact that everyone can have whatever it is that they want, those resources of abundance that are available all around us, is what benefits us the most as we are moving forward.

The stone used here is the Labradorite stone. This protective stone is highly mystical and a bringer of light. It raises consciousness and connects with universal energies. Psychologically, it banishes fears, and insecurities and the psychic debris from previous disappointments including those experienced in past lives. It strengthens faith in self and trust in the universe. It removes other people's projections, including thought forms that have hooked into the aura. Overall, the labradorite calms an overactive mind and energizes the imagination bringing up new ideas. This stone can be worn over the heart chakra, held and/or placed as appropriate.

Purpose of Transition Statement: Be receptive of the fact that everyone can have whatever it is that they want, and that resources of abundance are available all around us. Understanding this is what benefits us the most as we are moving forward.

The Lord Is My Light

The Lord is my light and salvation whom shall I fear Lord is the strength of my life of whom should I be afraid-Psalm 27
The Lord is my Law, my cause, light and salvation. The physical and spiritual laws of Life can have a transforming effect on your life. Take care of your body so it will take care of you is a physical law. Connecting to God in yourself and others is another spiritual law. You have the power to make your own happiness by what you think, say and do. You can attract things and add happiness to your life, world and affairs by treating your brothers and sisters the way you want to be treated. Let us be keepers of the light. Let us be conscious of being made in God's image and likeness. God is perfect, whole and complete; what's true about God has got to be true about you and me. I live my life treating others the way I want to be treated. I have nothing to fear
~The Spirit Within Colette Grant

Imani Faith

FAITH IS

Peaceful Practice

You can construct a very positive world for yourself or a very negative world with the power of your own words. Think before you speak. Think about the construction or destruction of the power of your words. Be aware that you have a very powerful force within and around you. There is a power in being aware. Be aware of yourself and your surroundings for it beholds great insight. How did you do with your words today?

TRANSITIONING INTO PURPOSE

Summer Solstice: New Transition Phase

⇆Retract if need be⇆

6
FAITH IS...[6]

Faith is the substance of things hoped for, the evidence of things not seen.
~Hebrews 11:1

THINGS TO CONSIDER:

Challenge Question: How do I stay in the NOW? Write down and explore those reasons thoroughly.

Affirmation: I transform my fear and anxiety in the process of conscious manifestation is by staying in the NOW.

Healing Crystal: Lapis Lazuli

This feeling of something shifting has been a constant feeling lately. In fact, it has caused a great level of anxiety. With the state of the world, anxiety has randomly been

---

[6] **Inspired by:** Eckhart Tolle

Imani Faith

at an all-time high. My ears have been ringing and I have felt this tingling feeling from my crown going down the spin of my back. Seeing all synchronized numbers, 111, 222, 444, 777. There was this headache I could not seem to shake and subsequently I became extremely exhausted. It was like I know, feel, and see everything that I need to do, but the more I think about it or try to focus, it becomes overwhelmingly heavy. I tried having a glass of red wine, even tried taking a couple of pulls of my favorite sativa hoping it would calm me, but it did not work. I felt full, thinking, "if only I one more of me." The actuality of that was impossible. I needed balance.

    I know, you've been at a point of being overwhelmed too. What I learned is, we must remain focused on what can be done NOW. Focus on what is happening NOW. Know that

TRANSITIONING INTO PURPOSE

the NOW is working with you and not against you, even if you find yourself unhappy.

Is your desire and your pattern of thought in sync? The key is to not get stuck on the physical of what is but focus on the emotions of what are. Tapping into that which you feel fuels your true desire, therefore allows you to control your thoughts, as a result creating a physical response. Always feel what you want whether you can physically see it or not. In simpler terms, I recalled the times that I woke up stressing about something in which I had no control of at the current moment. The stress created an unhappy emotional reaction that then created a chain of negative emotions. This turned into was a web of confusion.

Imani Faith

It was not until I shifted my thoughts, that the deep overwhelming feelings left. The key is to keep the unwanted things deactivated.

However, should you find that unwanted unconsciously activated itself, immediately activate that want. This can be done by thinking the opposite of what you actually are experiencing. So, if it's being unhappy, focus on happiness. If it's fear, focus on trust. If it's anxiety, focus on being calm and so forth.

Purpose of Transition Statement: I've stated this before, but it is important to remember these thoughts. Focus on what can be done NOW. Focus on what is happening NOW. Know that the NOW is working with you and not against you, even if you find yourself unhappy.

The two stones I used here were Lapis Lazuli and Black Onyx. Lapis Lazuli is also a protective stone that is the key to spiritual attainment. It recognizes spiritual attacks,

TRANSITIONING INTO PURPOSE

possesses enormous serenity, quickly releases stress, brings deep peace and contacts the spirit guardians. It also teaches the power of the spoken word and can reverse curses or disease caused by speaking out in the past. It is a stone that harmonizes the physical, emotional, mental and spiritual levels. This is a stone that encourages taking charge of life, reveals inner truth, encourages self-awareness and allows self-expression without holding back or compromising. Overall, this stone is a powerful thought amplifier, stimulates the higher facilities of the mind, and brings objective and clarity. Lapis Lazuli can be placed at the throat or third eye and should be positioned above the diaphragm anywhere between the sternum and the top of head. The Black Onyx is a strength giving stone that assists with challenges in life, especially energy draining

Imani Faith

situations. It helps to purge unwanted energies and passively helps with wand healing, increase stamina and self-control. This stone can be worn or placed on the left side of the body or around the neck.

A Prayer

Be patient and wait on God. Saying this, at a time, of calmness, and Solitude, at one time, and my life, were just words.
But the power of these words did not magnify themselves in my mind until I was face-to-face with something I was told, was called an opposite force "In boxing language, your opponent" this may sound like a joke, but you really have to fight with yourself to be patient. But, it is even harder to fight for those, who are now in the reality, of the existence of God.
I also fill my mind with the words of Trust and believe that God will see you through.
Trusting and believing to me is the inspiration of faith. Faith that He will see you through your darkest hour. Faith that he knows what's good for you. Faith in the belief and the power of prayer.
I would like to say an inspirational prayer for you. A prayer that helps you keep a light shining in my head and heart.
Oh! Holy Father Grant me Health and Peace
Teach me how to take care of myself
Teach Me How to Love You So I may find myself in You because
We are one!
~The Spirit Within Colette

TRANSITIONING INTO PURPOSE

Peaceful Practice

Speak Out Loud: My God gives me a challenge sometimes only to keep me mentally sharp, respectfully strong, and in harmony with some of life's invisible forces. My God is humble, my God is health, my God is prosperity. I am an heir to all of God's goodness and wealth. Amen. Repeat and rewrite until this gets in your spirit.

Imani Faith

TRANSITIONING INTO PURPOSE

Autumn Equinox : New Transition Phase
⇋Balance⇋Stability

7
SEASONS[7]

Every day is a new day to be great!

THINGS TO CONSIDER:

Challenge Question: I challenge you to live the life you want to live, free from being controlled by anything. What if anything has the most influence over your life?

Affirmation: I will remain committed to my purpose, I will not waiver.

Healing Crystals: Diamond and Aventurine

During times of the unknown, these inescapable happenings that stretch us beyond our capacities are something that we can all take a second to learn. Instead of succumbing to the storm, or focusing on the negative aspect of the storm, realize the energy

---

[7] Inspired by Les Brown and My own Family & Friends

that has occurred because of the storm. Could you imagine what beautiful things that will come after the storm? What if you have to start over? The important thing is to acknowledge the disconnection. The purpose is to feel good and watch what happens. After that, you can shift, focus on the good, and watch the results.

I consciously choose to go outside of my comfort zone and not be concerned about what people would think. I decided that my life has so much meaning to the planet and realized that I have something to give. That is why I exist. Like you, I'm on a journey and have a destination, mission, to achieve, to implement, to perform, and to experience. I make a daily decision to go forward and allow life to inspire me.

I challenge you to commit yourself to live in the present. Commitment means no excuse is

TRANSITIONING INTO PURPOSE

acceptable. Make it a priority. Find something that is manageable; start small if you have to. Should you break your commitment, own it, evaluate and access what happened, and if all is well—keep going, reset, reboot. If necessary, do a tradeoff or deny yourself of something, that is meaningful to you. We learn from experience. Build up the courage to become committed. Do not put yourself in a position where you give up on your commitment. Do not volunteer your life solely to others. Be so strong that nothing can disturb your peace of mind.

    I chose to honor my commitment as myself. You must decide that for yourself as well! Choose results over giving yourself reasons to not make progress.
It's truly an amazing and humbling experience to witness transformations take place right before ones' very eyes.

Imani Faith

    The sacrifices that were made while studying the mind and how it relates to one's spiritual, physical, and emotional well-being have been essentially rewarding. As I laid in bed giving gratitude to the Most High God, I couldn't help but reflect on some core lessons learned this year while tapping into self. Being that there was a time that I would consider myself one to quickly react based on mood and emotionality, learning to control my thoughts became the highlight of my spiritual work within self. As I continue to reflect, this way of living could have equaled my demise. There were times when I would take on the burden of others and allow their burdens to consume me. There were countless days I experienced loneliness and sadness, causing me to question myself and my identity. I would go into hibernation in order not to feel overwhelmed. I

TRANSITIONING INTO PURPOSE

had to regroup, secretly hoping that I would receive the support I gave. I am now mature enough to go full force at tackling my emotional triggers in order to remain fully aligned.

I've progressed to the point where the doubt and negativity are no longer welcomed in my headspace nor is anything else that doesn't serve the purpose of protecting my peace. For growth, I am eternally grateful! I thank the Creator in advance for the gift of emotional attunement!!!

The crystal I suggested here for your own increased health are the Diamond and Aventurine stones. The diamond is a symbol of purity and commitment. It is an amplifier of energy and one of the few stones that never needs recharging. It has been a symbol of wealth for many years and is one of the stones of manifestation, attracting abundance.

Psychologically, the diamond imparts qualities that include fearlessness, invincibility, and fortitude. Its positive healing properties include the unification of the mind and body. It also activates the crown chakra, linking it to divine light; further benefiting the brain by stimulating creativity, inventiveness, imagination, and ingenuity. This crystal is best placed near the skin, particularly near the skull or worn as jewelry. Aventurine aids in prosperity, friendship, and benefits all areas of creativity.

It provides a sense of calmness, balance, positive outlook and courage. Aventurine protects your energy from those around you, and further it enhances happiness and inner strength. When wearing the aventurine stone, it is important to know that it absorbs electromagnetic smog and protects against environmental pollution, basically diffusing

TRANSITIONING INTO PURPOSE

negative situations and turning them around. It can be worn, held or placed appropriately.

Here are a few lessons learned thus-far from my experiences involving loved ones that could be beneficial to you as well:

1. Don't take it personal
2. Everything is not meant to be understood
3. Simply love and allow others the freedom to be who they are
4. There are endless ways of seeing things and doing things, remain flexible
5. Identify when and who to nurture
6. Don't question what you already know
7. Know when and who to express yourself to
8. It's ok to forgive and ask for forgiveness to salvage a meaningful relationship
9. Know when to let go
10. Trust the process

FINAL THINGS TO CONSIDER:

What's my purpose again?
Affirm: I use my energy to heal and manifest as I transition into purpose!

Purpose of Transition Statement: Use your energy to heal and manifest as you transition into purpose!

Imani Faith

We Unfold To New Beginnings

*We walk up the path to a New World of New Beginnings.
Courage, Peace, Love, Patience, Understanding, Faith! The new world is within
The Spirit Within is having many beautiful babies.
The body calls them cells of Health, The Spirit calls them cells of Wealth
Look! Look! Over there where? Over there
Hi! My name is Peace, What's yours?
Love
Come meet understanding
Hi! This is Courage and this is Forgiveness, and this is Kindness, and this is Wisdom, and this is Patience, and this is my very good friend Faith. HAY! Don't forget about Me Who's me? Me Truth
We couldn't forget about you; we strive and live off of your fruit.
~The Spirit Within Colette*

TRANSITIONING INTO PURPOSE

Peaceful Practice

Don't become too embedded into old habits if you want to experience true change. Think on new good habits and then begin to act it out. See a picture of where you are going. What are some actions you want to change? Record them below.

Pray this aloud: Heavenly Father, strengthen my determination to disregard negative habits. Help me to replace them with positive habits.

Contact The Author

Do you want to schedule a book signing or speaking event with the author?

Complete the contact form at www.imaniisfaith.com

www.ingramcontent.com/pod-product-compliance
Lightning Source LLC
Chambersburg PA
CBHW072048160426
43197CB00014B/2681